This book belongs to:

Managing Editor
Mara Ellen Guckian

Editor in Chief
Brent L. Fox, M. Ed.

Creative Director
Sarah M. Fournier

Cover Artist
Kelly McMahon

Art Coordinator
Renée Mc Elwee

Illustrator
Kelly McMahon

Imaging
Amanda R. Harter

Publisher
Mary D. Smith, M.S. Ed.

Edupress
A Division of Teacher Created Resources, Inc.

12621 Western Avenue
Garden Grove, CA 92841
www.teachercreated.com

ISBN: 978-1-4206-0168-8

Reprinted, 2021

Made in U.S.A.

Edupress™
A Division of Teacher Created Resources

Introduction

The letters of the alphabet make different sounds. The relationship between these letters and the sounds they make is known as *phonics*. This is a book to help young learners identify some of the sounds that letters make as they practice tracing and printing them. On each page, young learners are asked to identify a picture, say the word, and listen for the beginning, ending, or middle sound. Then, they trace and write the word.

Note: When helping read the directions, pronounce the sound the letter makes when it is presented between backslashes. For instance, when you see /b/, say the sound "buh", not the letter "b".

How to Use Pages 3–14

In this section, encourage your child to identify each picture and listen to the beginning sound of the word. Then, have them trace and write the word on the lines provided. If you wish, have them circle each beginning letter.

How to Use Pages 15–25

The focus shifts to *ending* consonant sounds in this section. Continue identifying each picture, but this time, focus on listening to the ending sound. Then, have your child trace and write the word on the lines provided. If you wish, have them circle each ending letter.

How to Use Pages 26–30

This section focuses on the sounds made by each of the short vowels—*a, e, i, o,* and *u*. There is a page to introduce each short vowel sound. Using the picture clues, have your child listen for the middle sound—the short vowel sound. Then, have them trace and write each word. If you wish, have them circle each middle sound.

How to Use Pages 31–32

Use the final pages of *My First Phonics Book* to review some of the sounds and letters practiced throughout the book.

Beginning Sound - Bb

Trace and write the words that begin with the /b/ sound.

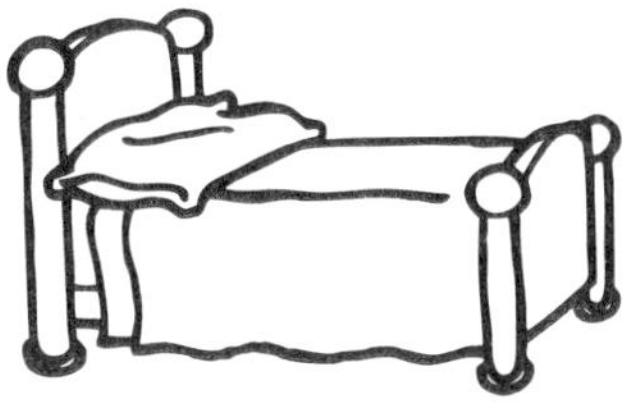

bed

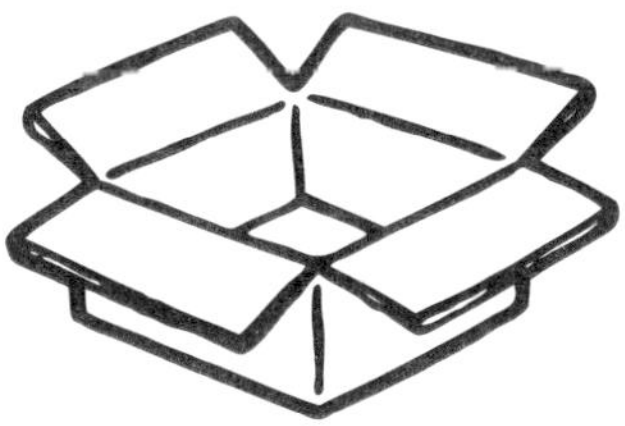

box

bus

bat

Beginning Sound – Cc

Trace and write the words that begin with the /c/ sound.

car

cot

cat

cup

Beginning Sound – Dd

Trace and write the words that begin with the /d/ sound.

dog

doll

duck

dip

Beginning Sound – Ff

Trace and write the words that begin with the /f/ sound.

fin

fox

fish

fan

Beginning Sound - Hh

Trace and write the words that begin with the /h/ sound.

hen

hat

hot

hut

Beginning Sound – Jj

Trace and write the words that begin with the /j/ sound.

jam

jet

jug

jar

Beginning Sound – Mm

Trace and write the words that begin with the /m/ sound.

mug

men

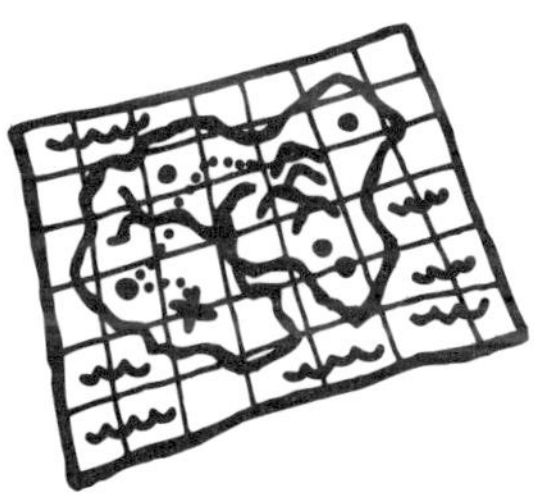

map

mom

Beginning Sound – Pp

Trace and write the words that begin with the /p/ sound.

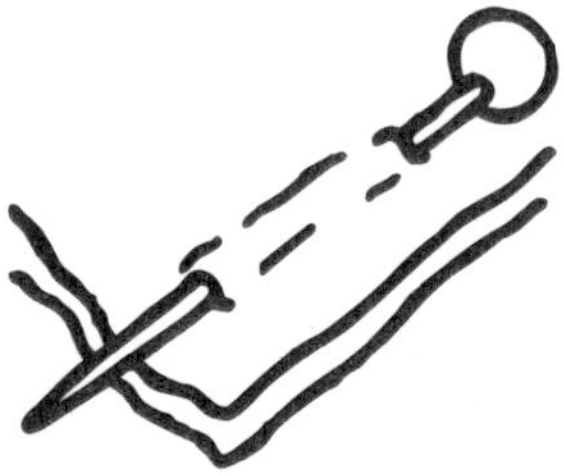

pin

pot

pan

pod

Beginning Sound – Rr

Trace and write the words that begin with the /r/ sound.

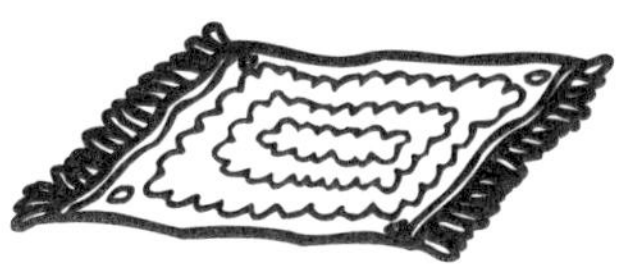

rug

rip

run

rat

Beginning Sound – Ss

Trace and write the words that begin with the /s/ sound.

sun

sub

six

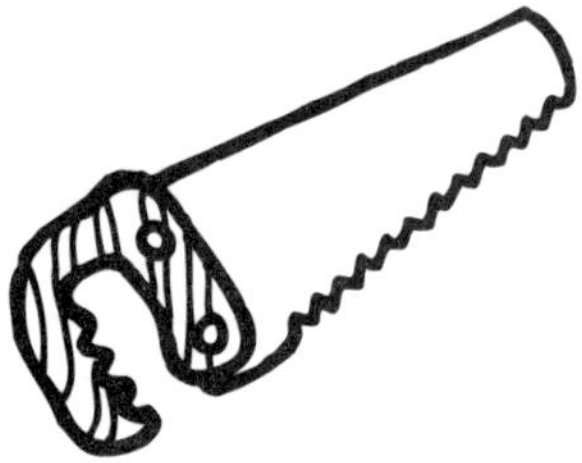

saw

Beginning Sound – Tt

Trace and write the words that begin with the /t/ sound.

tub

tag

top

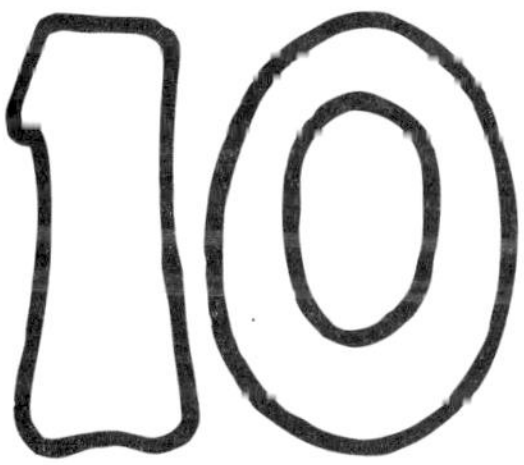

ten

Beginning Sound – Ww

Trace and write the words that begin with the /w/ sound.

wig

web

win

wet

Ending Sound – Bb

Trace and write the words that end with the /b/ sound.

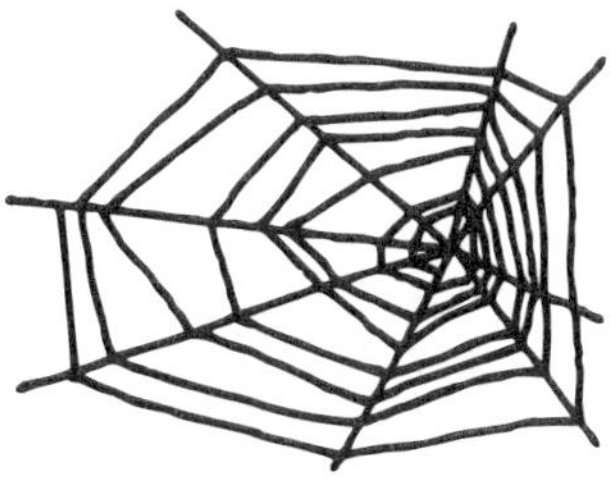

web

bib

tub

crib

Ending Sound - Dd

Trace and write the words that end with the /d/ sound.

bed

dad

mud

pad

Ending Sound – Gg

Trace and write the words that end with the /g/ sound.

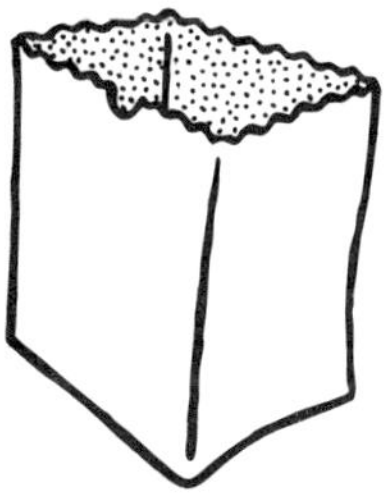

bag

dog

pig

bug

Ending Sound - Ll

Trace and write the words that end with the /l/ sound.

ball

bell

doll

bill

Ending Sound – Mm

Trace and write the words that end with the /m/ sound.

jam

gum

mom

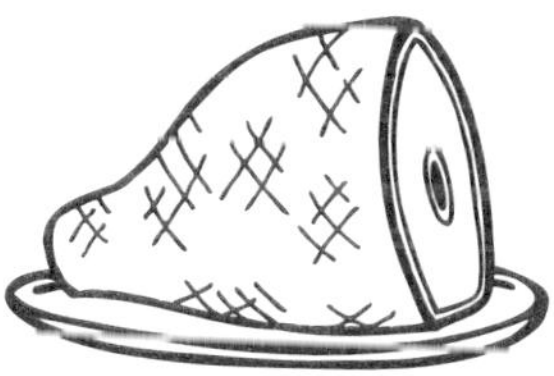

ham

Ending Sound – Nn

Trace and write the words that end with the /n/ sound.

fan

sun

pin

pen

Ending Sound - Pp

Trace and write the words that end with the /p/ sound.

cup

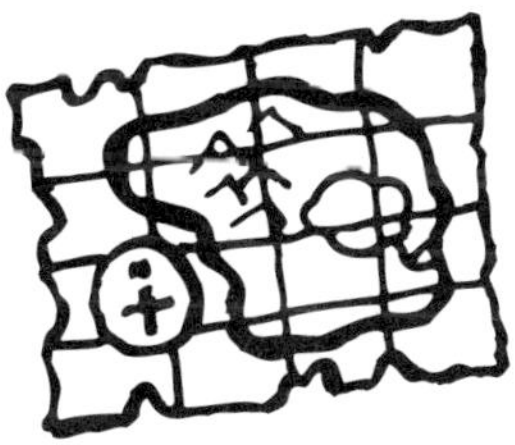

map

zip

mop

Ending Sound - Rr

Trace and write the words that end with the /r/ sound.

jar

car

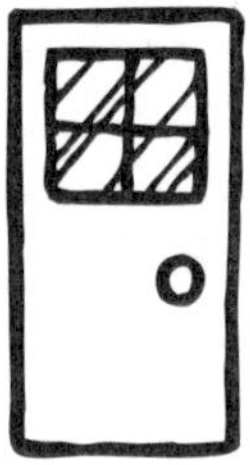

door

four

Ending Sound – Ss

Trace and write the words that end with the /s/ sound.

bus

gas

yes

kiss

Ending Sound - Tt

Trace and write the words that end with the /t/ sound.

cat

jet

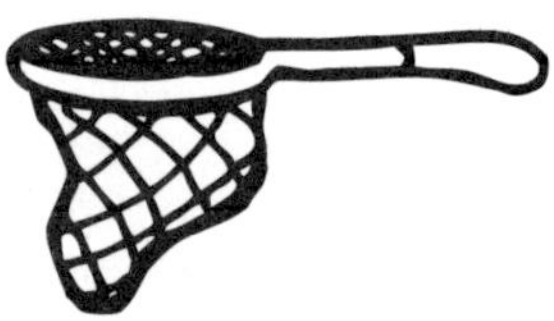

net

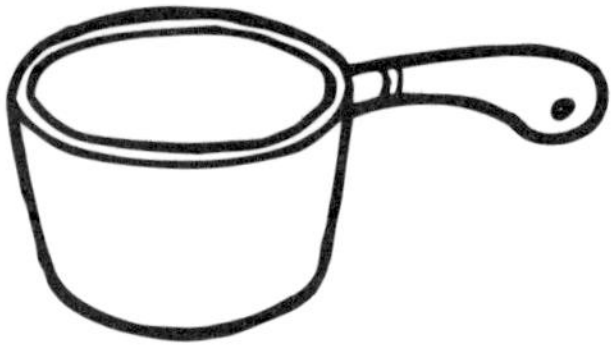

pot

Ending Sound - Xx

Trace and write the words that end with the /x/ sound.

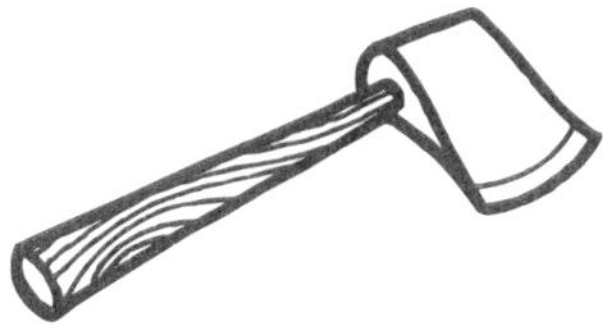

ax

six

ox

fox

Middle Sound – Aa

Trace and write the words that have the /a/ sound in the middle.

van

gas

nap

bat

Middle Sound - Ee

Trace and write the words that have the /e/ sound in the middle.

vet

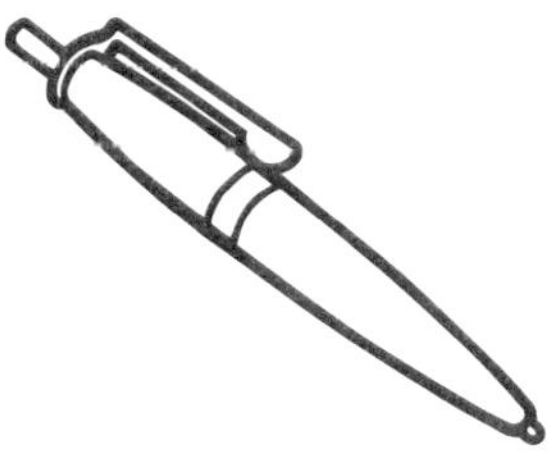

pen

bed

web

Middle Sound – Ii

Trace and write the words that have the /i/ sound in the middle.

bin

dig

bib

pin

Middle Sound – Oo

Trace and write the words that have the /o/ sound in the middle.

top

box

mop

pot

Middle Sound – Uu

Trace and write the words that have the /u/ sound in the middle.

nut

tub

rug

bus

Change the Beginning

Trace the first word in each row. Write the beginning letter to finish spelling the rhyming word next to it.

tag

ag

jet

et

wig

ig

top

op

cub

ub

Finish the Words

Name each item and look at the letters provided. Fill in the missing *beginning*, *middle*, or *ending* letter to complete each word.

 ma_	 s_b	 _en
 b_n	 po_	 _an
 _ug	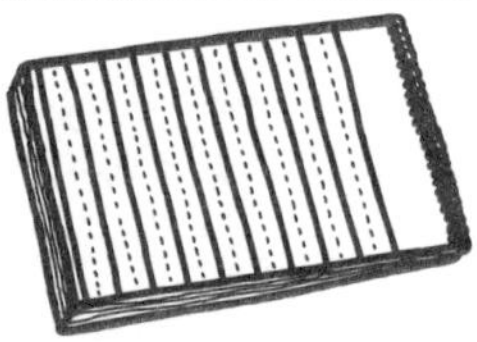 pa_	 h_t